July 2007

Staircase Poems

Alice Lyons

For Bebe, Bob, Julie, Mike, Ruby, Lonie,

With love,

Alie

we had a beautiful time with you at the Vineyard

A PUBLIC ART PROJECT AT:

The Dock
St. George's Terrace
Carrick-on-Shannon
County Leitrim
Ireland

3

Published by:

The Dock in association with Leitrim County Council
under the One Percent for Art Scheme

ISBN:0-9553950-0-3
ISBN: 978-0-9553950-0-0 (after January 2007)

Photo pp. 24-25: Reprinted with permission of the National Archives, Dublin
Photo pp. 40/42: Cyril Byrne, *The Irish Times*
Photo p. 42: Steve Woods
Installation photography: David Knight, Roscommon
Other photos by the author

set·in Adobe Jenson Pro 14/11

Designed by: pure
Printer: Craftprint Group, Dublin

www.alicelyons.blogspot.com

The Dock
St. George's Terrace
Carrick-on-Shannon
County Leitrim
071-965 0828

The Department of Arts,
Sports and Tourism

Contents

Forward

The Dock is a multi-disciplinary arts centre installed within the shell of Carrick-on-Shannon's former courthouse, an impressive 1,400sqm (15,000ft) building dating from ca.1822.

The building has a spacious double-height front foyer, leading into a larger triple-height stairwell incorporating a wide granite stairs of 18 steps. The Dock's three galleries are all at first floor level and there were concerns that their location up this granite stairs would demand an extra commitment from the casual visitor to the building. They might be satisfied that their visit to The Dock has comprised the Café / Bar and Leitrim Design House on the ground floor, they might wonder (in a relatively austere building) whether they are supposed to go up the stairs at all, or they might have decided from the ground floor that the art in those galleries just wouldn't be for them.

The renovation of the building was well under way when I took up post in November 2004, but the public art feature (arising out of the Dept. of Arts, Sport and Tourism's Percent for Art Scheme for the building) had yet to be commissioned. I initially wondered whether we should commission a public art work of elaborate chandeliers, fibre-optic loops, or reaching sculptural forms that would begin in the front foyer and disappear into the ceiling of the stairwell; drawing the person who happens through the front door to follow these strands and be led into the triple-height space so that their journey up the stairs to the galleries would seem a natural and easy progression.

At the end of November 2004, I found myself involved in the *Artist-as-Traveller* project, which had arisen out of Cliodhna Shaffrey's time as Curator-in-Residence in Leitrim. Part of the project incorporated an exhibition spread throughout various rooms in King House, Boyle. Alice Lyons' work stood out for me; a film poem entitled *Blow In, County Roscommon*. This film poem was not on a wide screen TV, or projected large onto the wall, but on the screen of a laptop computer in a small basement cell, really only for one viewer at a time. It was deliberately intimate, as if Alice were initiating a conversation with each person who stood before it. The animation of the lines of the poem on and across the screen was deliberately playful, and while the questions asked were directly of the artist, they were sincere, and appreciable by anyone who would happen in there.

Some weeks later I was again standing in the building-site/foyer of The Dock looking skyward, still trying to figure out how best to incorporate a public artwork. I was no longer convinced of the potential of chandeliers or fibre-optics. The more I thought about it, the less the idea of a permanent piece of art seemed

to fit with the place. Not only would such a piece date a building that we want to continuously re-invent, it might also colour people's expectations about the kind of art on show or just be in the way of other art projects (somewhat defeating the point of an arts centre).

I remembered really enjoying the work *For Dublin* by Frances Hegarty and Andrew Stones (IMMA's Nissan Art Project in 1997). Their collaborative work involved presenting extracts of Molly Bloom's monologue from James Joyce's *Ulysses* in bright neon lettering around prominent locations in Dublin City Centre, like City Hall and along the Liffey wall. (Maybe it was thinking about the fibre-optics that brought this piece in neon to mind). I liked that the content sought to connect directly with the city, I liked how carefully each site was chosen to suit each extract, and I liked how you would happen across it, like an unexpected gift. But I also liked the idea of artists, backed by a state institution, provoking us - to smile and think *'what do we know?'*; to notice where we are and think *'where are we at?'* It seemed like a perfect example of the kind of artist-led projects that any healthy democracy should be promoting.

In the building-site/foyer looking skyward through scaffolding, remembering bright neon Dublin parlance, considering what The Dock should be, how that might be made real, and how a public artwork might support it all, Alice Lyons'

film poem in the small cell in King House came back to me.

I hadn't met Alice, but knew enough to trust the possibility. The rest of the idea unfolded quite quickly, because it seemed such an obvious fit – poems commissioned for the staircase changing throughout the first year of The Dock's life, making that which might have been the hurdle act as the bridge; work commissioned for our hinterland, because we want to be relevant to that hinterland; a voice to humanise an old courthouse and initiate a new dialogue with people, and that the primary voice of The Dock would be the voice of the artist.

But it is difficult to imagine that anyone else might have engaged as faithfully, as generously and as successfully with this project as Alice has. She has a deep appreciation for this part of Ireland and the people who live here. Her capacity to appreciate us and our place may derive, in various parts, from the sensibility of the poet, of the artist or of the person from New Jersey who lives in Cootehall (that *Blow In, County Roscommon*). But she is unquestionably of us; and so too are these *Staircase Poems*.

Caoimhín Corrigan,
Arts Officer

7

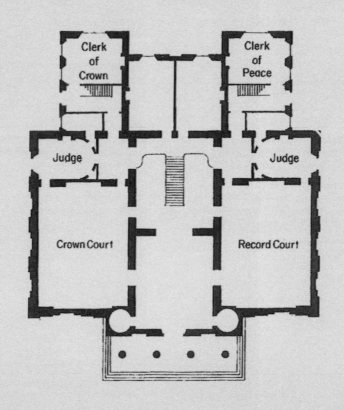

1

Make Good All Existing

Match original lime harling render.

All existing to be made good.

Keep, salvage, strip, paint, repair.

Enclose tunnel access for prisoners to old

Gaol with c̶o̶n̶c̶r̶e̶t̶e̶/̶s̶l̶a̶b̶ steel grate.

Overhaul, take down, cart away, keep leve

Open up. Hack off. Rake out. Reinstate.

Drains to be back-filled with river grave

MAKE GOOD ALL EXISTING

Séan said, *No, I never had reason*
to go into THAT *place, thanks be to God.*
He cocked a calloused thumb
at the hotchpotch of scaffold
(dread word!) and blue hoarding:
Carrick-on-Shannon Courthouse
where a poem is constructing
itself in the architects' general notes.

    MATCH ORIGINAL LIME HARLING RENDER.

    ALL EXISTING TO BE MADE GOOD.

    KEEP, SALVAGE, STRIP, PAINT, REPAIR.

    ENCLOSE TUNNEL ACCESS FOR PRISONERS TO OLD

    GAOL WITH CONCRETE SLAB STEEL GRATE.

    OVERHAUL, TAKE DOWN, CART AWAY, KEEP LEVEL.

    OPEN UP. HACK OFF. RAKE OUT. REINSTATE.

    DRAINS TO BE BACK FILLED WITH RIVER GRAVEL

COMMENTS

Poem should be
about Leitrim no
Roscommon!

12

2

The Cleaheen Road

The Cleaheen Road

The intensity of the Cleaheen Road
it has always been so, walking it
   last night in the wind every neutrino
      kinetic. Each beech tree leaf
      shook by berserk puppeteers.
         Lughnasa chasing the skirts
            of late summer air
            willows sizzling, rustling crinolines
            and the river gets all confessional
            says the mist was just a fling
            her cold slit Giotto virgin
   blue and unflinching.
A gust sets down for a moment
   in the plastic pound shop chair
   the Germans put at the edge of Lough Eiden
   then rushes off to the party
   of sky and wind and water
   between here and the Hill of Usna

where Thomson walked the back way
to the Bawn with Phoebe, yet
another romantic tragedy.
Rolls of silage in the fields
emphatic, entitled hulks
displacing space
as if they deserved to be more loved
as if the moving world
the vectoring wind
revolved around them
on the Cleaheen Road
near the village of Cootehall
where the tongue forever stumbles
and is heard a brute word
hissing in such fleet voices
of long ago local girls
listen for them
of County Roscommon.

THE CLEAHEEN ROAD

The intensity of the Cleaheen Road
 it has always been so, walking it
  last night in the wind every neutrino
   kinetic. Each beech tree leaf
    shook by berserk puppeteers
     Lughnasa chasing the skirts
      of late summer air
       willows sizzling, rustling crinolines
       and the river gets all confessional
      says the mist was just a fling
       her cold slit Giotto virgin
      blue and unflinching.
    A gust sets down for a moment
   in the plastic pound shop chair
 the Germans put at the edge of Lough Eiden
then rushes off to the party
 of sky and wind and watr
    between here and the Hill of Usna
     where Thomson walked the back way
      to the Bawn with Phoebe, yet
       another romantic tragedy.
       Rolls of silage in the fields
      emphatic, entitled hulks
     displacing space
   as if they deserved to be more loved
  as if the moving world
    the vectoring wind
      revolved around them
     on the Cleaheen Road
       near the village of Cootehall
        where the tongue forever stumbles
         and is heard a brute word
        hissing in such fleet voices
        of long ago local girls
       listen for them
      of County Roscommon.

shocking! shockin
shockin' shockin'!

16

3

Dirty Weather

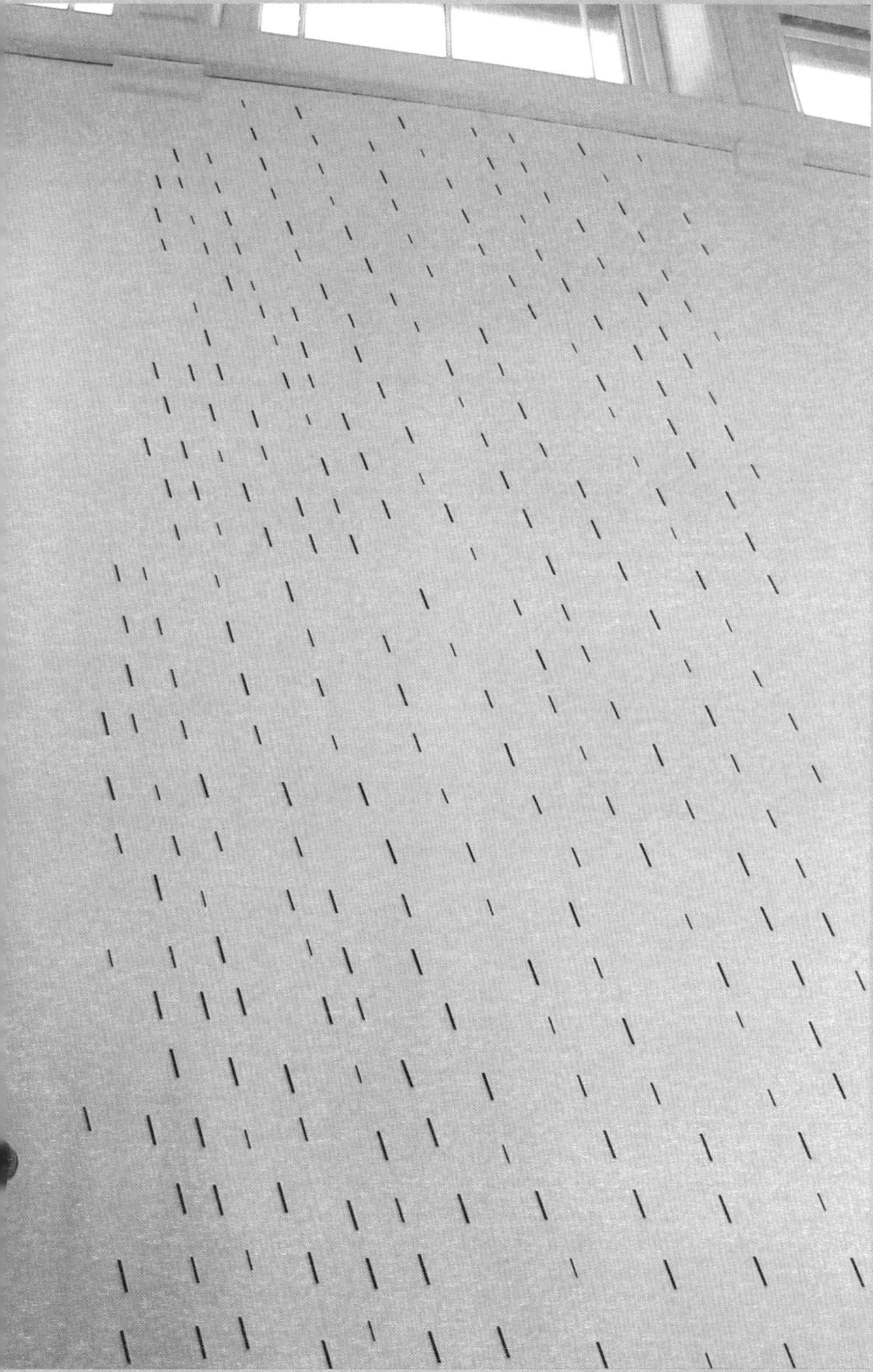

Dzień dobry. Nazywam A...
jestem Amerikanką

Miło mi panią poznać.
(Nice to meet you)

Mnie też miło pana poznać.
(Nice to meet you too)

4

Żaden Bestseller
No Bestseller

before tears fall?

ŻADEN BESTSELLER

NO BESTSELLER

Z tego wiersza nie będzie żaden bestseller.
I am writing no bestseller.
Bardzo możliwe że tylko mojej córce
Chances are only my daughter
będzie się chciało przeczytać
will care to read
te słowa po mojej śmierci.
this when I am dead.
Jakże mam jej (lub tobie) wytłumaczyć
How can I explain to her (or you)
że nigdy nie widzę wyraźniej
why my sight is never clearer
niż w tym wezbraniu, w tej
than in the welling up, that
wypukłej chwili nieskończonego zwielokrotnienia tuż
convex moment of infinite extension right
przed wypłynięciem łez?
before tears fall?

Polish translation by Justyn Hunia

Reynolds — P   Edwd Do ————   w   Arthur Do   P

Donaghe — P   Bryan Do ————   w   Peter Crow

—ulay — P — John Do ————   w   Francis Reynolds—

—Tate — P   Catherine Gennerty — w   Mich Do ————

Flynn   w   John Flynn ————   w   Denis Blake

Reynolds   P   Wm Reynolds noted orphans w   Bryan Kelly —

Fox   P   Patt Reynolds   w   Mich Crogan

Flynn   w   Patt Conaner   w   John Kelly —

Reynolds   w   ════════════   Bryan Do

═══════════ C Amagh Edgeworth ══   John Blake

—woods   w   Daniel Cohany   P   Michael Duignan

—Donnelly w   James Do   P   Patt Crow ——

—Donnelly w   Lauun Cane   w   Denis Blake ——

—Donnelly w   James Kelly   P   John Caroll —

—canning P   Edwd Do   w   Mathew Reynold

Do ———— w   Patrick Reynolds P   Charles Blake

—Guichenan Thomas Do —— w   Edwd Brady

—w of Mich do w   John Do ——— w   Bryan Gumin

—& Maxwell —— w   Mich Heslin   w   Bridget Do

—ich Donaghe — P   Paul Heslin   w   Widow Reyno

—ll Slevin noted w   Patt Fox   w   ═══════════

—an Conafty —— w   ════════════   C Drumherk

—ell Duignan —— w   Amaghacunny   Con O'neil

—dow Guihoy —— w   Francis Cohany P   James O'ne

   Mich Heslin ——   w   James Do

Mc Keon — P	Thos Smith — w	
" Glancy — w	Edwd Cohany — w	
.d Grey — w P	Patt Reynolds — P	Nicht [...]
Ferry — w	James Do — P	Patt [...]
ick Grey — w	John Murphy — w	Wm O Loughlin
	Patt Canning — P	James [...]
[...]	Phelix Reynolds — P	Francis Mc Cole
itholemy Fox — w	Widow John Reynolds — w	John Crausting
Gunsheman — P	Widow Kelly —	w Hugh Reynolds
Do — P	James Rogers — P	Wm [...]
Reynolds — P	Widow Duignan — w	James Kerr
Gihay — w	John Roach — P	[Turnablad]
Glancy — w	Owen Murphy — w	John Duignan
Duignan — P	Patrick Woods — w	Jo Do Jr
Do — P	Bartly Foley — P	John Do Sr
M Cohany — P	Patt Murphy — w	John Do
Do — P	Ellen O Neill — w	Hugh [...]
Fox — w	Francis Reynolds — w	Bryan [...]
Doran — w	Francis O Neill — w	John Do
		Daniel Rogers
ngrania :	Gun	Widow Reynolds
Rogers — P	John Reynolds — w	[...]
Flynn — P	Patt Cohany — w	Patt Glancy
Bohan — P	Michael Reynolds — w	William Killaghin
Roork — P	Matthew Cohany — w	Mich Rogan

"Loughwrinn Union List – With an accurate acct of this townland and the names of persons seemingly distressed for subsistence living on said farms in the electoral division of Loughwrinn together with placing the letter P at the foot of every mans name where plenting appeared and placing the letter W at the foot of the distressed mans persons name which signifies want. Dated this 22nd of March 184

Poem graphically represents this census in Leitrim relief Commission papers, National Arch

nt want want want want want want want want want want want want
nty plenty plenty plenty plenty plenty plenty plenty plenty plenty plenty plenty
nt want want want want want want want want want want want want
nt want want want want want want want want want want want want
nty plenty plenty plenty plenty plenty plenty plenty plenty plenty plenty plenty
nt want want want want want want want want want want want want
nt want want want want want want want want want want want want
nty plenty plenty plenty plenty plenty plenty plenty plenty plenty plenty plenty
nt want want want want want want want want want want want want
nt want want want want want want want want want want want want
nty plenty plenty plenty plenty plenty plenty plenty plenty plenty plenty plenty
nt want want want want want want want want want want want want
nt want want want want want want want want want want want want
nty plenty plenty plenty plenty plenty plenty plenty plenty plenty plenty plenty
nt want want want want want want want want want want want want
nt want want want want want want want want want want want want
nty plenty plenty plenty plenty plenty plenty plenty plenty plenty plenty plenty
nt want want want want want want want want want want want want
nt want want want want want want want want want want want want
nty plenty plenty plenty plenty plenty plenty plenty plenty plenty plenty plenty
nt want want want want want want want want want want want want
nt want want want want want want want want want want want want
nty plenty plenty plenty plenty plenty plenty plenty plenty plenty plenty plenty
nt want want want want want want want want want want want want
nt want want want want want want want want want want want want
nty plenty plenty plenty plenty plenty plenty plenty plenty plenty plenty plenty
nt want want want want want want want want want want want want
nt want want want want want want want want want want want want
nty plenty plenty plenty plenty plenty plenty plenty plenty plenty plenty plenty
nt want want want want want want want want want want want want
nt want want want want want want want want want want want want
nty plenty plenty plenty plenty plenty plenty plenty plenty plenty plenty plenty
nt want want want want want want want want want want want want
nt want want want want want want want want want want want want
nty plenty plenty plenty plenty plenty plenty plenty plenty plenty plenty plenty
nt want want want want want want want want want want want want
nt want want want want want want want want want want want want
nty plenty plenty plenty plenty plenty plenty plenty plenty plenty plenty plenty
nt want want want want want want want want want want want want
nt want want want want want want want want want want want want
nty plenty plenty plenty plenty plenty plenty plenty plenty plenty plenty plenty
nt want want want want want want want want want want want want
nt want want want want want want want want want want want want
nty plenty plenty plenty plenty plenty plenty plenty plenty plenty plenty plenty
nt want want want want want want want want want want want want
nt want want want want want want want want want want want want

Thanks for stopping

And for the chat.

6

Memorandum in Winter

Rhymes with her face, an

To consult before engagi

Thanks for stopping. And for the chi

Then she's a dot

MEMORANDUM IN WINTER

Cutting the engine
When meeting her on the boreen
Me in my Volkswagen diesel
She with her push-bike
She with her plaid shopping satchel
That billows like a windsock:
Memorandum of my smugness.

A tangled extravagance
Of whitethorn and briar
Rhymes with her face, an opened map
To consult before engaging the gears.
Thanks for stopping. And for the chat.
Then she's a dot
In the rear-view mirror.

7

Things I Didn't Know I Loved

uong traffic cones. (There's an underlyi

idit know I loved shadows,

ones stone walls cast, how the

ked path to pick along.

t know I loved her parties de-bus

lervous Animals versus Drumshanbo

now I'd come to love the

, rumour and neighbour

THINGS I DIDN'T KNOW I LOVED

I didn't know I loved the street dogs of Boyle
every one, equal parts scruffed-up and old-souled
or that there was a reliable gang
of plasterers available to me at reasonable rates
if only I'd ring.
I didn't know I loved funerals, certain funerals,
how a village whips into action, Hi-Vis vests donned,
someone yells, *Joe! Priest car!* , and it's directed
among traffic cones. (There's an underlying passion.)
I didn't know I loved shadows,
the ones stone walls cast, how they map
a forked path to pick along.
I didn't know I loved hen parties de-bussing at the chapel
or Those Nervous Animals versus Drumshanbo Gun Club.
I didn't know I'd come to love the "u"
in *colour, rumour* and *neighbour*
or how when a friend from Aberdeen says *odd,*
it sounds, to these ears, like *awed.*

(after Hikmet)

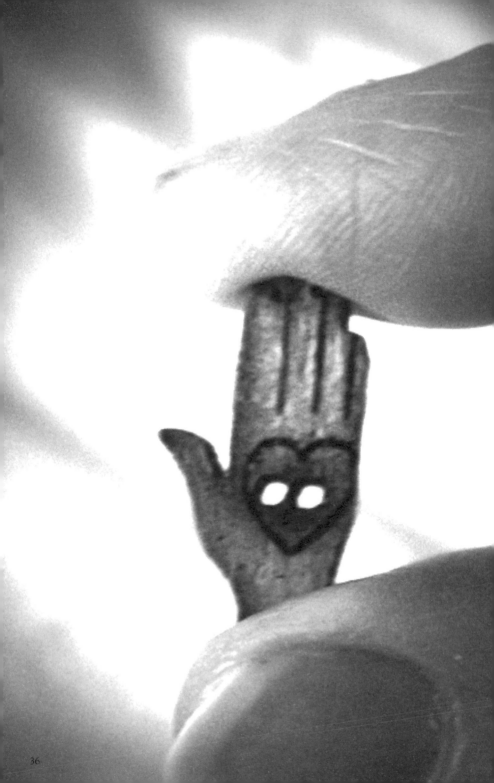

8

A Story From Effrinagh

The rope was made of flax.

+ + + +   + + + + + **+** + + + ☞

Retrieval is an art.

She saved the piece of rope.

That yanked his life apart.

A STORY FROM EFFRINAGH

He dangled in the air.
The rope was made of flax.
The trial wasn't fair.
He dangled in the air
Beside the courthouse where
The truth got mauled by facts.
He dangled in the air.
The rope was made of flax.

+

Retrieval is an art.
She saved the piece of rope
That yanked his life apart.
Retrieval is an art.
The cure worked on the heart
With flax and words and hope.
Retrieval is an art.
She saved the piece of rope.

9

Photograph of Mister Justice Feargus Flood

AN CHÚIRT

PHOTOGRAPH OF MISTER JUSTICE FEARGUS FLOOD

(*The Irish Times,* day of publication of the Tribunal's second interim report)

They say the left eye
tells the truth
(it's closer to the heart
some profess).
That leaves the right
for what you want
us to believe, for
your version of events.

This left eye's hooded
clammed-up, inward
keeps its own counsel
spots bullshit from a mile.
The right one laughs—
as if some wise
guy just emerged
from the long grass.

10

Caution Staircases

caution staircases

elevate everybody

make individual footfall music

create displaced persons

cannot be goosestepped up

give hope to middle managers

act like baby magnets

make nowhere somewhere

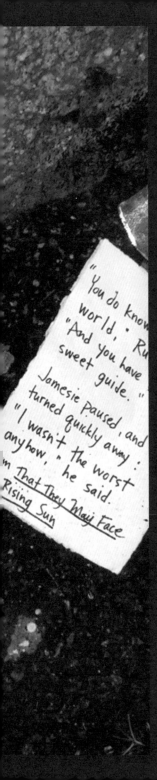

11

Report

On
the
radio
the
politician
said
Memoir
made
him
cry
for
his
own
early
losses.

Chris
said
it
was
heavy
going
and
finally
she
couldn't
hack
it.

The
dentitst
said
he
thought
your
man
was
a
depressing
old
so
and
so
and
why
bother

Mary
said
she
wasn't
sure
she
was
up
to
reading
it.

The
RTÉ
television
newsreader
said
*Ar
dheis
Dé
go
raibh
a
anam
dílis*
before
moving
on
to
the
next
item.

The
text
message
simply
read
MCGAHERN'S
DEAD

Lila
said
she
had
never
met
McGahern
but
he
was
a
lovely
man. MIKE
SAID
HE
SHED
A
FEW
TEARS
READING
IT
IN
*THE
IRISH
TIMES*
EXCERPT.

blowin local   an

lilac b

lac bowl

cow
own
coal bill
lilac
bowl
wino
allow
bacon
clown
clan
bawn
icon
nail
loan
law   all

How Blow-ins Become Locals

twelve HOW BLOW-INS BECOME LOCALS

My senior infant makes out the message

on a Denny's rasher truck : HOME

IS WHERE YOU MAKE IT

And we pass them again

They're filing out the Leitrim Road

bending into the rain like willows

Kurds heading for *Lis Cara*

under a useless golf umbrella.

Hey, there's our Kurds!

Last night our swallows blew in

from Africa, chirruping in a disused shed.

Our willie wagtail's local

and mighty territorial.

Then there's the conversation at a gate

near Drumkeerin : *My hippie's cuttin' hay.*

What's your hippie at today, so? So

it begins — the circuit of us.

HOW BLOW-INS BECOME LOCALS

My senior infant makes out the message
on a Denny's rasher truck : HOME
IS WHERE YOU MAKE IT
And we pass them again
they're filing out the Leitrim Road
bending into the rain like willows:
Kurds heading for *Lis Cara*
under a useless golf umbrella.
Hey, there's our Kurds!

Last night our swallows blew in
from Africa, chirruping in a disused shed.
Our willie wagtail's local
and mighty territorial.
Then there's the one heard at a gate
near Drumkeerin: *My hippie's cutting hay.*
What's your hippie at today, so? So
it begins—the circuit of us.

Biography

Alice Lyons was born in Paterson, New Jersey and grew up in the United States. In 1998, she came to live in Cootehall, County Roscommon. Her work embraces poetry and visual art.

Her first unpublished collection of poems, *speck*, won the 2002 Patrick Kavanagh Award for Poetry. In 2003, she received a bursary in literature from the Arts Council, and in 2004 she was chosen by Nuala Ní Dhomhnaill to receive the inaugural Ireland Chair of Poetry Bursary. Earlier work received an award from the Academy of American Poets in 1981.

Lyons' poems have appeared in *Poetry Ireland Review*, *Stand* magazine, mermaid turbulence's *element*, *The Shop*, *Barrow Street*, *Tears in the Fence*, and *Dancing With Kitty Stobling* (Lilliput Press, 2005). Her paintings and drawings have been widely exhibited and are in the collections of the Office of Public Works and NUI Galway. Her film-poem, *Erasures*, won the award for best first film at the Sligo Short Film Festival, 2005.

She studied European History at Connecticut College (B.A. 1982), Sociolinguistics at the University of Pennsylvania (M.S. 1988) and Painting at Boston University (M.F.A. 1994). She lectures in Art & Design at the Galway-Mayo Institute of Technology.

She was commissioned by Leitrim County Council to write this series of poems to be installed as public art on the staircase of the Dock from August 2005 through August 2006.

Thank You

Every poem is some sort of public art project. If you could hold up to a bright window pane the real paper on which a poem is written, you might see the names of all the people who inhere in that poem as a kind of watermark. That is certainly the case with this poem project and this book. Those named here and many more that I have regretfully neglected to include are part of the supporting fabric of these poems. Go raibh míle maith agaibh and thanks a lot:

Anne Fletcher & Luise Volschenk of Coady Architects, foreman Robbie Fox, Constantine Jura & the rest of the construction crew of P.J. McLoughlin and Sons, John O'Donoghue, T.D. Minister for Arts, Sport & Tourism, Elizabeth McAvoy at the National Archives, John Bredin & members of the Carrick-on-Shannon Historical Society, Justyn Hunia & Dorota Cisowska in Kraków, Barbara Stachura in Warsaw, Paddy Doyle, Sister Tomasina & all members of the Carrick Active Age Group, medical & nursing staff at Sligo General Hospital and Richmond Ward, Beaumont Hospital, the people of the village of Cootehall, Yvonne Bauer, Siobhán Garrigan, Norma Gottlieb, students & staff in the part-time Art & Design painting course at GMIT Cluain Mhuire and Castlebar campuses, Sheila Pratschke & staff at Tyrone Guthrie Centre at Annaghmakerrig, Nuala Ní Dhomhnaill, Philip Delamere & Arts Office of Roscommon County Council, Ros Kavanagh, Thomas Repetowski, Donal Spring, Dave Donohoe, Mary Rafferty, Mike Burke, Christina Rafferty, Mari-aymone Djeribi, Dominic Stevens, Eibhlín Níc Eochaidh, Helen O'Leary, Paul Chidester, Frankie Watson, Gerry Bambrick, Johnny Markey, Séan & Mary Higgins, Afke Pieterse, Will O'Hara, Kate & Pat Ryan, Katy & Diarmuid Delargy, Fergus Delargy, John Brady, Fionna Murray, Austin Ivers, Cliodhna Shaffrey, Michael Ewing, Megan Woods, Steve Woods, Maryanne & Ray Lyons, Jane Lyons, Michael Stoner, John Albert Duignan, Laura Gallagher, Rose McGovern, Lila Holt, Bernie Phillips, Joan Gallagher, Ann Gibney, Bernie Giblin, Tim Gilbride, Anna-Maria O'Rourke, Geraldine Gray, Patricia Holahan, Joan Lowe, Finola Lavin, Joseph Gilhooly, Danny McLoughlin, Terre Duffy, Paul O'Gara, Martin Reading, Claire McAree, Liz O'Dowd, Brendan McDermott, Úna Wall, Manus McManus, Siobhán O'Malley, Hazel Walker & Denise Lyons. Mark O'Reardon, Darach O'Broin, Colin Elliott & all the staff at Silverstone sign makers in Dublin provided excellent service and vinyl. For generosity with time and creativity, many thanks to Linda Shevlin and Padraig Cunningham – Pure Designs. Caoimhín Corrigan instigated the idea of poems on the staircase and as such has been invaluable collaborator throughout. I extend grateful acknowledgements to all the members and staff of Leitrim County Council for their support and encouragement of this project.

For Caoimhe

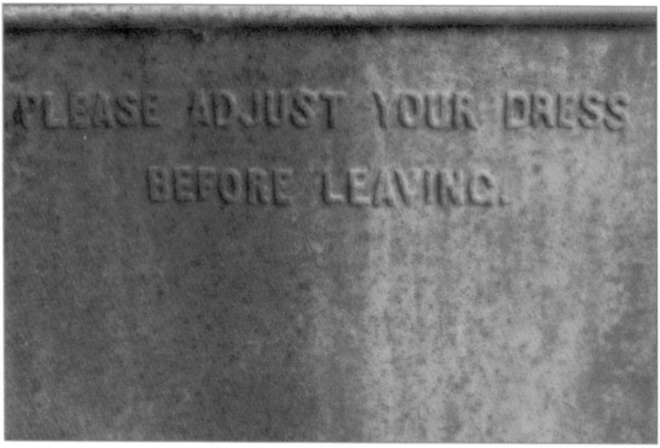
PLEASE ADJUST YOUR DRESS
BEFORE LEAVING.